THE GIFT OF COUNTRY LIFE

Victor Carl Friesen

NATURAL HERITAGE BOOKS
TORONTO

Published by Natural Heritage / Natural History Inc.
P.O. Box 95, Station O, Toronto, Ontario M4A 2M8
www.naturalheritagebooks.com

All colour photography is by the author; black and white photographs are from the author's collection unless otherwise identified.

Library and Archives Canada Cataloguing in Publication
Friesen, Victor Carl
        The gift of country life / Victor Carl Friesen.

ISBN 1-897045-07-7

1. Farm life — Saskatchewan — Poetry. 2. Country life — Saskatchewan — Poetry. I. Title.

S522.C3F75 2005   C811'.54   C2005-904305-9

Cover and text design by Sari Naworynski
Edited by Jane Gibson
Printed and bound in Canada by Hignell Book Printing of Winnipeg

Canada Council
for the Arts

Conseil des Arts
du Canada

ONTARIO ARTS COUNCIL
CONSEIL DES ARTS DE L'ONTARIO

Natural Heritage / Natural History Inc. acknowledges the financial support of the Canada Council for the Arts and the Ontario Arts Council for our publishing program. We acknowledge the support of the Government of Ontario through the Ontario Media Development Corporation's Ontario Book Initiative. We also acknowledge the financial support of the Government of Canada through the Book Publishing Industry Development Program (BPIDP) and the Association for the Export of Canadian Books.

To the memory of my mother, Anna Friesen

CONTENTS

INTRODUCTION: Hay Bales   *10*

SPRING: Homecoming   *13*
                   Encounter   *15*
                   Conjunction   *17*

SUMMER: Two Horses Grazing   *21*
                   Branched Out   *23*
                   The Mowing   *30*
                   Well Digging   *35*
                   Watering the Cows   *38*
                   The River   *45*

FALL: Leaf Fire   *67*
                   The Meadow   *69*
                   Sawing the Winter's Fuel   *72*

WINTER: Winter Evening   *85*
                   Survival   *87*
                   Skiing   *88*

AFTERWORD: Tribute   *97*

ABOUT THE AUTHOR: *109*

INTRODUCTION

I was born and raised on a quarter-section farm (160 acres) near Rosthern, Saskatchewan. This was mixed farming country so that a typical farm had its forty-acre cow and horse pasture, a large yard with barns and pens for chickens and pigs, an equally large vegetable garden, a hay meadow somewhere, and about a hundred cultivated acres for crops. There was a great variety of work, and amusements, for a farm boy.

My birth year was 1933 and my growing-up years the 1940s, before farming became the highly technical, big-time operation it is now. Haying was still done with a mower and rake drawn by two horses, and the hay put up in stacks (the horses would also pull our buggy and wagon in summer and bobsleigh and cutter in winter); livestock were watered at a bucket-and-pulley well, hand-dug in those days (ours was a quarter mile from the yard because our household pump well went dry periodically); crops, such as they were on sandy land, were cut with a binder and stooked in fall (a separator and lively crew came out to thresh them, leaving straw stacks in our field or pasture); and dried trees were cut and hauled home to be sawed up for fuel for the kitchen range and living-room heater. My father and older brother hauled logs as well from ravines along the South Saskatchewan River.

The highlight of each summer was a fishing trip to the river, six miles away, providing food for the table and a break from the usual workaday routine. Winters in the '40s decade were cold and blizzardy enough that from Christmas to Easter I worked at my high-school correspondence courses at home and sought amusement in skiing, on homemade skis, across the country in the blue of evening, always observant of the colours of snow and the wildlife flourishing about me.

Things changed rapidly after mid-century. Mechanized equipment made for larger land holdings, doing away with a lot of neighbourly effort in getting jobs done. Farms became electrified and modernized with plumbing and the latest home appliances. Country schools closed and children were bused to town for their education; social activities came to be centred in towns, too. The pace of life quickened and community spirit was not so localized as before.

For me personally, the changes were also marked. My father died in 1950, and an auction sale the next year ended our farming operation. Since I had then completed grade twelve, I left the farm to attend normal school and, the following autumn, began my teaching career. My siblings, older than I, had already gone. Mother also left, for the city to do day-work in winters. But the farm was not sold. It was always there for us to return to.

Mother was the most faithful to the home place, going back each spring, as soon as the snow melted, to resume her country life, a gift she would not relinquish. To her it was the best place to be — even without electricity and running water. She enjoyed getting water from the squeaky pump at the well and lighting a coal-oil lamp. She prided herself on having a small workable hand that could squeeze inside a lamp chimney with some crumpled paper to clean it — that made a squeaky kind of sound, too. Ever the farm ....
She died in 1988.

It has been said that you can take a boy out of the farm but you cannot take the farm out of a boy. Eventually I bought the land where I was born, not willingly letting go of country life either. Although I now live in Rosthern, just five miles away, I go "home" to renew my inner being, to think clearly those thoughts that tend to get muddled in my brain in an urban setting. And there are always some puttering jobs or relaxing things to do —

mowing the yard, pruning the trees, walking nostalgically to the hay meadow, sensing the great night coming on.

The seventeen poems here, describing this rural world, are mostly in traditional blank verse, grouped into seasonal activities or observations. The circle of the year, after all, is the essence of country life. About a third of the poems detail activities of the older way of farming, another third focus on my puttering work of the present day, and a final third hail eternal nature, ever the same, which links all country life together whatever the era. Nature, as Henry David Thoreau has said, is "one and continuous." Fittingly, the last poem, as a separate afterword, deals with both past and present times as well as their ongoing relationship to nature, in tribute to the one who most appreciated *The Gift of Country Life*.

HAY BALES

Farm cows at ease about their winter's hay,
drawn from round, solid bales amid the snow,
recall, if dimly, in their bovine brain,
far pastures summery with smells and now
time-capsuled by each bale's slow chemistry.

SPRING

HOMECOMING

Walking to the empty farmyard
with the spring night coming on — an
April evening coldness there, and
daytime's fluffy clouds but dark, thin
carded remnants floating by — I
pressed through poplar saplings, sprung from
garden plots unplowed alongside
aspen bushes, and unmowed, too.
Dirty snow lay thick in swatches,
molded, scalloped, melted down, left
from the sculpted drifts of winter,
crystallized about the saplings,
crunched and shattered by my steps.

                                  Thus

I approached along a path that
led up to my home of boyhood
(and of birth): the greyed house standing —
still as it had stood, deserted
but not lonely, so I thought, with
ageless trees about it (planted

in an ell that marked a lawn), with
dense adjoining thickets closing
in upon the yard, snug woodland
haven of ruffed grouse and hooting
owl. The old house seemed at peace in
the pale light of dusk, at one with
Nature and acclimated.

                Now
darkness settled in at last, on
yard, the trees (fusing their limbs), the
greying house that loomed against the
sky: a honking, then, of migrant
geese in slanted skeins, sailing low
over the wood and calling softly
each to each and flying onward
through the night; and stirrings elsewhere,
as I listened, of raccoons that
shambled from the house before me —
theirs, presumably, and mine (and
something to be shared)— a welcome,
in a way, to stay and visit.

ENCOUNTER

Dusk. April night descending.
A cold mist greying things.
Distant bushes blurred, obscured.
Last year's grasses sodden at my feet.
Somewhere, a faint hallooing.
A wild crying, maybe. Voices.
Silence again.
I, huddled, still, peering into dimness.
Nearer clamour then.
A muted *honka-honk.*

A lone goose in cleaving flight
emerges darkly from the mist,
(had it heard my far-off steps
and come to reconnoitre?),
swings wide in parabolic arc before me —
just one acknowledging brief *honk*—
and surges swiftly back
through veils of space and mystery
to some safe rendezvous
with others of its kind.

CONJUNCTION

The evening calm that led me out of doors
before retirement and bed, with but
an hour left to end this warm spring day,
became for me a time to breathe the cool
moist air, to feel the brief night coming on,
to sense from this tomorrow's cherished weather!

There, in the dim northwest, perched just above
the blackened aspen bush, an orange slip
of moon about to set soon vanished from
my view. As the new moon descended, touched
the tips of trees (a jewel poised), somewhere
a sparrow sang, a buzzing trill, as if
whole darkness hardly deigned to fall here in
this northern night — the distant clouds still glowed
with brownish tones, the remnants of a sunset.

But all the lower world was jet, save where
a solitary firefly traced out
its slow and steady course with spots of light;
then honeyed fragrance, velvety, surged up

(as from a resting, still, deep-sleeping earth),
the scent of silverberry or wolf-willow.

The evening calm that led me out of doors
let all sensations merge for one great time:
a moon, new-bent, now nestled in the trees;
a small clay-coloured sparrow's buzzy song;
a firefly's lit trail in pitchy dark;
the welling up of fragrant willow musk!
All these may never come at once again,
may never come to end a warm spring day,
may never come again for us to cherish.

SUMMER

TWO HORSES GRAZING

Two horses grazing in the meadow — one
a bay, the other buckskin-yellow — shake
the buzzing flies from their sleek, sweated backs
with a quick shudder. Half a twitching hide
and half a deep and rolling rumble in
their throats send gnats and green-eyed dung flies up
into an angry cloud that settles on
a rump. But then a stamping hoof protests
upon the sod, and all the tail that has
no central bone whips forward, sending the
bedeviled horde to reconnoitre. And
the horses pause but little in their job
of urgent eating. How their busy lips
blubber about the succulent green grass!

I knew a red cow once that ate till its
four legs seemed foreign to itself and their
small size incongruous with the great trunk
ballooning out in bloated agony.
That night the farmer led her round some sloughs,
hearing the night cry of shorebirds and the

deep booming *thrum* of some fat frog, wondering
if exercise would keep his foolish cow
from bursting. Circling night-encompassed ponds
again and yet again, he pondered this.
"I hope she'll be all right, the silly thing."

But horses are distinct from cows. They're smart.
The buckskin horse will nibble only till
the bay lifts up his head and gazes at
the wavering horizon where the sun's
light shimmers from a leafy bush (the wind
is silent in the grass). Now shuffling up,
he'll droop his head across the other's back,
and both their ears will twitch and turn to hear
the dung flies buzzing at the dusty heat.
Farm horses are a well contented lot.

BRANCHED OUT

"The evil that men do lives after them ...."
Will Shakespeare's right but also other than
the way that he intended. Uninterred
are influences shaping later lives,
for sequences will have their consequences.

It was a bright warm summer day, my thoughts
high up among the ordered row on row
of rained-out clouds, I paused to reason thus.
The earlier deluge of rain, coming
the night before, and the great wind that brought
the downpour to its end had also brought
down branches from the planted trees about
the yard — long glass-like limbs of poplar that
are called "water" or "black" to mark them from
the native aspen; brittle twigs of maple,
the Manitoba kind (box elder is
its other name); and tangled trunks of one
that's said to be a shrub, but hardly so,
the caragana — its one name's enough.

"We'll plant the maples close together, and
the wall they make should save the inner yard
from winter's snow, at least the curving drifts."
So spoke my father to my older brother.

"And just in case some die, we'll plant still more
along the north side." This my brother said.

It was the nineteen forties, still the time
of lingering thirties' drought when withered brown
was summer's colour, that and dried-out yellow.
The prairie grass burned brown, a greyish-brown
in August heat, and crops bleached whitish-cream.
The caraganas from an earlier
quick planting had remained true shrubs — how could
they grow, their leaves lost by the last of each
July? Trees and more trees were needed then
to overwhelm the drought and make the world
say "Green," to make one farmer's heat-parched yard
an Eden, an oasis — refuge and
a strength, a place poetic — all its trees
in leafy verdure lovelier than poems.

And so the trees were planted with a will.
What was worth doing was done well, so well
the seedling maples all gave out before
the north side was completed — needing room
to grow seemed no real reason, then, that limbs
just sapling branches, could almost touch
each other. Black or water poplars, scrounged
from neighbours' yards, were used to fill the gap.
The job was done, and maples, poplars, and
the caraganas stood in steadfast rows
in a triumvirate of trees, each kind
with its unique advantage. Poplar, now,
was fastest growing in real drought conditions;
the maple bushed out in a cluster; and
the caragana had its sturdiness.
So let the brown and yellow yard be green.

My father died; my older brother left
the farm; the rains came down — all this one year.
The rains, held up for thirty years (the years
my father farmed) continued to come down
for summer after summer. Thirty years
(and more) it rained to match the thirty years

of drought: the grass was green; the crops were green;
the trees reached up and grew in time gigantic.

Advantage turned to disadvantage. The
black poplars soon expended growing strength
in suckers, shoots, and runners, while the trees
were towering to seventy-foot heights.
Just too much growth for days of seasoning —
a slightest wind, a rain, or heavy snow —
and branches shattered, hurled from high, and strewed
the yard, and all with waxy buds that stained
the hands and stuck in pads when underfoot.
The Manitoba maples grew in bushes —
the pruning came too late — so that each trunk
was slanting upwards while the limbs always
were slanting down: the pruning never ceased.
Meanwhile, new shoots sprang out, and others dried
and broke away, and little bladed seeds
spun earthwards, there to start the whole process
anew. The caraganas, too, grew up
with slanted trunks that reached *towards* heaven, but
it could be said, the thirty feet of growth
(and that diagonal) was not the kind

to lead one up in spirit or in body.
Frost's birches they were not, for boys to climb
up on and then swing down. Instead, they broke,
and that from their own weight, each one subdued
in ignominious display, with tops
entangled, intermeshed, a thicket. Worst
of all, the dried seed pods split open, spewed
out kernels for another cycle still.
The nearby bluffs of native aspens soon
were jungles, choked with caraganas — no
wild fruits or woodland flowers or a log
within a clearing where the ruffed grouse drummed.
A good day's flailing with an axe made just
so little headway, with no room to swing,
the chopper stood disastered, sweaty, out
of breath and out of sanguine hope to win.
Before I'd plant a tree, I'd like to know
just how it grew and if its branches lay
in wreckage after every storm. Of course,
my father and my brother could not know
the future. All they wanted then was but
improvement, something green and flourishing,
edenic in a world gone wrong.

                                   Now here
I am, three decades past, the world's aright,
but this one "garden's" out of kilter. With
each fallen branch I stoop to gather, I
begin to wonder whether this small plot
can represent a small improvement on
another, or a great refreshment to
one's spirit (Bacon holds a garden is
the purest form of human pleasure). But
I know I've had too much of picking up
of branches. I am overtired of
this useless harvest, and my thoughts dwell on
the blameless "evil" of the planting of
the trees (if so it may be called) back then.
For even unintended evil lives
long afterwards to change our lives. It is
when I am rested that I welcome each
tree's shade and sound of branches, coolness in
the air. But now, right now I've had too much of trees,
of fallen branches lying twisted in
the grass. I'm tired, overtired, and
my weary mind comes back to deeds done by
my father and my brother and left now
for me to right. They could have planted spruce.

Author, in boyhood, busy with camp chores at nearby South Saskatchewan River.

Four mowers working in the July heat,
two men and two machines paired each to each:
one mower tractor-driven by its man,
cutting a ten-foot swath of long-stemmed brome,
which falls in overlapping, swishing piles
around the outer yard on this old farm,
deserted now save for the haying time;
the other mower pushed by hand, its man
walking behind within the twenty-two
scant inches shaven clean, amid the bits
of greenish mulch spewed on the inner lawn
that lies beneath an ell of maples all
around the house itself.

                Each pair that mows,
machine and its accompanying man,
describes in circles of mechanic noise
the progress of the day — the tractor hums
and whirs, trailing a clicking blade that cuts
a set of hesitant and incomplete
short radii of some gigantic wheel.

The little mower on the lawn stutters
and pops and alternates its roar — from fierce,
where grass is tall or thick and seems to need
intimidating — to persistent, where
the harebells bloom and scented roses do
not signify a threat. The rotary
blade cuts every one.

               And so the work
proceeds, each mower making wheels or rings
of fallen grass or flowers, circles and
more circles, each concentric to the other.
The little mower's "wheels" within the ones
laid by the larger tractor-mower — and
the smallest circle, seeming central to
them all, is cut each moment by the small
pushed mower's still revolving blade. Yes, wheels
and turning wheels, each swath that's cut is meshed
with ones before — a synchronized grand plan,
which drones along (or bores ahead), for such
are modern times.

And then at some fixed time,
as if all preordained, the two machines
both stop, their whirring sounds cut short, and in
the sudden silence welling round, now from
the tractor steps the ten-foot man —"descends"
might be a better word — and meets halfway
the other man, he of the twenty-two
scant inches, counterpart to him. The first
hulks down upon the grass and twaddles with
a lengthy stem of brome he snatched along
the way; the second plumps right down and chews
a leaf to see how it might taste. It is
a time to talk and humanize the day.

The first, in overalls, has come from home
across the road to salvage hay from the
deserted yard by rental — his four cows
were winter-fed from here last year. In slacks
and T-shirt, and of course with half-chewed leaf,
the second sits, back from his city job
to tend on weekends homestead chores that he
has fallen heir to: mowing the yard,
a city-dweller's kind of haying (yet

it might be said, by some, such work is but
a way of playing at the age-old role
of husbanding the land).

                       No matter, he's
content this day to quit the city world
and dwell on country things. If work is play,
the talk is real: "The crops are not too bad";
"They still could use another rain, that's sure";
"How are the farmers' gardens hereabouts?"
"The new potatoes should be ready soon."

Author's mother with Dutch hoe in backyard garden. Author was born in this house, 1933.

A man stands tall before an open well —
he stands and waits, Miltonic in his pose,
the pulley rope held loosely in his hands.
And one below, in darkness it would seem,
works, troll-like, at his trade within a pool
of seeping water, shovel in *his* hands.
The first looks down into the pulsing depths —
which send the cold reflections rippling up
against the curbing, capturing a bit
of sky where only enclosed blackness was —
and realizes a great stature in
his tired body. Not that he's become
taller because the well grows deeper, nor
could tugging at the rope have stretched him — much.
Thus pondering, he either waits or hauls
up earth in this two-man attempt to dent
the earth's circumference. His hands are white
with clay on roughened skin from the worn rope.
The rope's resistance or persistent pull
against his pulling says why transfer earth,
why not best leave the wet earth where it was.
But bucket after bucket comes on up,

Old bucket-and-pulley well.

is dumped in slithering mud pies — oh, just
a children's game, he thinks, bemused; some mud,
tenacious, that won't leave the pail but must
go down again to start another load.
And rubber-footed, sluicing mud into
the bucket, squats the other man. "All right,"
is echoed up the well, and up the pail
ascends with drops of water dripping down.
The well becomes a bucket deeper, too.

When wells are deeper still, it's said that from
their daytime depths, which give what might be called
a tunnel vision, stars are to be seen
by the lone man within who's looking out.
A night sky seen beyond the well's round rim
that catches sunlight in its mouth — without
the silence of the trees, which hold the dark
in every leaf (and one bird not asleep)—
seems contradictory to nature's way.
Sun-bathed and sweaty, one man squints into
the darkened well, the world beneath his feet,
and one, frog-footed, cold and double bent,
strains up his neck and gazes at the star
that's shining in ethereal blue space.
Men looking up should have a star to see.

Throughout the spring and fall when school was out
and supper eaten, also at the end
of each long summer day, the farm boy's one
remaining task was watering the cows.
The well, hand-dug those days, was at the far
end of the farm, a quarter mile away.
These facts were prose, but the excursion was
for him poetic.

   "Josie, girl, come on,"
he'd say, and walk up to the leader of
the herd. The cows were lying down, content
with cud after the evening milking, and
the calves stood silently nearby, stopped in
their gambols by the boy's approach. Only
the smudge, to ward off flies, showed movement (with
exception of the cows' slow sideways chewing,
a tail's sometime reflexive flip); the smoke
itself dissolved into the quiet air
in tentative blue tendrils. Horses, two
in number, stood with heads above the smoke,
each resting on three legs, the fourth held limp.

"Come on," the boy repeated, and the cow
addressed, old Josephine, raised up her huge
and awkward bulk with a deliberate
submission, ambling to a well-worn path
that wound its way across the pasture. One
by one, the other cows lurched to their feet —
no word to them was spoken — and along
the narrow path, trod several inches deep
into the sod, followed in single file,
hooves clicking, heads now swaying side to side.
The calves strung out this caravan of cows,
as did the horses — all pursued the straight
and narrow — but just till the first real test
had interposed itself: a willow clump.
And there the path diverged, to left and right,
rejoined and left the willows islanded.
(No path in nature's straight, nor should be — it's
the narrow aspect that we need to keep
to.) On to aspens and their checkered shade
the path (and cows) continued; then across
some open hills, where hayfields were, each cow
in turn now silhouetted for one brief
moment against the setting sun before

descending to the well. The watching
boy descended last.

                      Already the five cows
were crowded round the wooden trough, nosing
the bit of day-warmed water there. The boy
then climbed the railing that enclosed the well,
opened the lid, and plunged the bucket down,
a moist, sweet coolness coming up from springs
below. The pulley hummed; the pulley rope
slid through the guiding hands, only to be
let go of altogether just at the
last moment — for the boy had learned to time
things right so that the bucket with a splash
would hit the water slantwise and submerge.
Now he peered down to watch it slowly fill.
Half-full was full enough — the boy had but
a boyish strength — and then the pulley squeaked
in rhythm to his pulling down upon
the rope hand over hand: a reaching up,
as if in supplication, to the sky
to draw from deep within the earth the gift
of water.

Cows on pioneer farm, anxious to drink.

When the bucket swung above
the open well, with water dripping down,
the boy reached over yawning space to catch
the bucket handle, careful all the time
with one hand on and holding back the rope,
the other outward, groping. Then, a quick
and swinging motion sent the water in
an arc out of the pail, over the rail,
safely into the trough. And best of all,
his feet were still on solid ground — something
he thought of with each bucket that he emptied.
(The pulley was a kind of balance with
the weight and strength of one farm boy opposed
to that of water and earth's gravity
behind it.)

Just on one occasion did
he overfill the bucket, had to let
it down in jerks, with hopes to empty it
again, to pay the well back once in kind.
But that he couldn't do — the water gave
the pail a fierce stability. Up came
the heavy pail once more in a droll game
of seesaw that the boy as soon would not

have played. What then?— prolong the game and send
the bucket down another time to see
if he, another time, could make it tip?
No, what was needed was a reach, along
with equal grasp, while staying earthborne, too —
no thought of heaven then: no thought at all
unless a moment's hesitation could
be called so. "Now or never" were his words,
and it was now — the game was at an end:
cold water in the trough, the boy on land.
Meanwhile, the golden western sky had changed
to russet red.

          Each bucket emptied from
the well released its dank earth odour, matched
the musty smell the meadow grasses gave
the evening air. Not all the livestock drank,
however, nor had all been drinking, for
the hierarchy within the herd, of which
the boy knew well, prevailed: the horses must
drink first. Thus Bruce, a spirited and dappled grey
young gelding, and old Tom, a lumbering
dark bay, now loitered at the trough. To drink
meant nuzzling the cold water just

as if their only motive were affection.
From time to time they raised their heads, with sheer
indifference to waiting cows — the cows
were simply shunted off (sometimes the grey
might even shunt aside the older horse).
But finally old Josephine, the cows'
own leader, exercised her bovine right
and *would* drink at the trough. The other cows
soon followed suit but butted back the calves
until the edge of their own thirsts was quelled;
then all could drink in democratic turn.
Such was the daily ritual seen at
the well.

      When all had drunk, the boy filled up
the trough against another day, then closed
the cover on the cool deep-delvèd earth
and strolled towards home. The cows by then once more
were grazing; nighthawks darted overhead,
their *peenting* call plucked from the night's steel cord.
The evening sky showed in the west a streak
of amber — up above, translucent blue
with one first-water star just coming through.

The man sat high upon the single disc,
was cantilevered to the rear with only reins,
or so it seemed, to pull him round the field.
In this surreal and earth-defying strange
display of sitting-levitation — the
loose overalls he wore hid the spring seat
and the flat, angled spring beneath it. Shoes
were dusty, dangling down; the pant legs and
the shirt, now black in every fold; the hat,
slouched low upon his head, soaked through with sweat.
The two bay horses, sleek with sweat themselves,
placed their great hooves down on the earth in short,
quick steps as if the soil were hot — it was —
and strained into their padded collars. Heads
bobbed up and down, hindquarters heaved with strength,
as this farm unit — man, machine, and beasts —
moved on with grating sound, a turning flash
of discs, confusing mix of horses' legs.

It was a scene Rosa Bonheur might well
have painted — horses with curved necks, flexed limbs,

and splendid muscles — or a scene that some
disciple of a Cole or Gilpin might
envision — with the team far down the field,
diminished in perspective, and a huge
white cloud behind it, cloud of summer bright
with sunlight, upswept to the heights of sky.
But on this day when man and single disc,
pulled by two horses, worked the sandy land
in serrate strips, then not a cloud was in
the sky, not even haze — the very air
seemed burned clean of all moisture, crystalline
in substance, so that distant objects were
defined as sharply as some artifacts
preserved through time and viewed through glass. For this
farm scene was not the pleasant countryside
of France, the misty Scottish highlands, or
the golden wooded hills of Hudson River.
Saskatchewan was what it was, the year
was nineteen forty-one, the only cloud
was dust from heat-parched soil, trailing the man,
the team, the disc. Perhaps the bottom curve
of each round blade knew coolness when it sliced
through crusted earth. If so, the dampness lurked

just in the dips of undulating field —
the slopes and rounded hills were powder-dry.
Yet grubs and a few beetles were unearthed,
and one lone gull accompanied the tillage.
It rose and fell in moveless flight, in arcs
that swept out sideways, then swung back into
the rising dust and landed briefly.

                                          Hot
and grimy, jarred upon the spring seat, rode
the man, grim, hopeless in his job when rains
refused to come. Short spumes of dust attended
each turning blade before him; horses' hooves
shuffled amid a welling up of dust
that constantly surrounded them. The air
smelled of this dust, smelled of his sweat and of
the horses' sweating — and nowhere at all
the rich, moist exhalation of good earth,
fruitful to man. For this one man there was
no seeming levitation of the spirit,
no inner strength left to defy the earth
and make it yield — just routine labour of
one day succeeding yet another day.

A four-horse hitch on adjacent farm, similar to that used by author's father for breaking new land on his farm. Note the seed drill at right.

He slouched upon his seat, disconsolate
to such extent he let each jostle of
the disc work through his body limply held.
What was the weary use, he thought, and this
his state of mind when it was barely noon.
There was a half day still to come with more
of horses' plodding, stifling dust uprising,
an out-of-place gull circling …

                              a lone gull!
He pulled the reins to stop — the dust both from
the disc and from the horses' hooves rose up
without its backwards trailing, and hung there —
and swung round on the seat to spy the gull
now hovering behind him, just above
the dust, wings arced, its whiteness gleaming (bleached
it seemed, but with a slight, faint texturing
because of layered depths of plumage), then
a giving way to soaring onwards as
its whim would so direct it, clean and pure
in every motion, effortless in flight.
The man sat gazing for a long time; then
he clucked his team and headed homeward, left

the disc at the field's corner, walked behind
the team up to the farmyard, past the barn
and to the pasture fence, untied the gate,
slipped off the harness from the horses, clucked
again and let them go. This done, the man
did up the gate, looped all the gear upon
the fence, and he himself strode to the house
for dinner.

       "Shall we gather at the river?"
the man, bemused, announced to wife and boy.
The two within the house looked back askance,
not understanding quite his meaning. She
had watched before from out the window, seen
what seemed to her his most unusual
behaviour, while the boy, not yet aged eight,
was wondering if a hymn were coming up.
"What ...," the wife started into say; she paused,
not knowing what her next words ought to be.
The boy looked from the mother to the father.
"I said," he said, repeating, "Shall we three
now gather at the river?" Here he paused:
"The river, Ansh"— he paused again —"I mean...."

He looked down at the boy, then at his wife
(her name was Anna, as you might have guessed):
"Let's go this afternoon." The boy of eight,
or nearly so, just swallowed once to catch
his breath, excitement in his eyes. The wife
looked quizzical and placed her hands upon
her hips; she shrugged and then held back a smile.
"Why not?" she said as if that settled it.

The preparations for the day's excursion
were an important part of this one day's
enjoyment, this escape from searing sky,
the stifling dust, and heated earth. The sound
of flowing water and the coolness of
a shaded bank were more than a retreat
from workaday routine — they were indeed
another world — just six miles to the east.
(The river, too, a practical farm voice
kept breaking in, was a provider for
the table.) After dinner, lunch was packed —
a loaf of homemade bread, a coffee jug —
the farm wife singing as she added eggs
and jam and butter from the well. The man

threw harness on another horse and backed
her to the buggy, while the boy crouched in
the scant, parched grass to gather 'hoppers, used
for bait. He stalked them as a hunter, tried
with small cupped hand to grasp them well before
they whirred away in flight: a bottle full,
held up aloft, for him already proud
achievement — this before the three of them —
man, wife, and eager boy — took their departure.

The father and the mother sat on the
one seat, the boy in back hunched on the floor,
each letting thoughts roam where they would that day,
not caring now to spoil the time with talk.
The buggy pony walked or trotted on
as was her wont; from slowly turning wheels,
cascaded down a thinnish stream of sand
behind them. Brier roses bloomed along
the wayside, as did pale blue harebells; from
the fence posts meadowlarks sang glees to all
the world; the sun continued to beat down
as mercilessly as before. But when
the distant hills across the river rose

above the blurred horizon, then the boy
stood up inside the buggy, gazed between
his parents' shoulders at that azured land
of far away, took notice of the long
and winding road immediately before
them, leading down among the scrubby hills,
ravines, and clumps of birch and poplar. He
now stood on tiptoe, wanting to be first
to glimpse the river through the trees.

                                 For most
of the descent, they followed a steep cut
down one side of a hill, the boy leaning
forwards and gripping hard the seat before
him — this, adventure in itself — the horse
now prancing but held back; then finally
a swinging off along a narrow trail
upon a wooded terrace just above the shore.
The horse with free rein broke into a gallop —
birch, aspen, willow, hazel branches scratched
against the buggy; those inside dodged limbs
of overhanging trees till all at once
horse, man, wife, boy, and buggy burst into

a grassy clearing with the friendly river
sparkling below. "We're here," the father said;
the wife relaxed; the boy already had
jumped down.

            It still was not a time to talk.
The man unhitched the horse and tied her to
a tree about which she could graze; the wife
took up the lunch and set it near a spring
to cool; the boy with fishing gear in hand
just stood before the water, looking ... looking ...
watched how the broad and fluid surface changed
unendingly, its flows enveloped by
still others; slicks of water moving to
and lost in meeting, rippled portions — all
sliding forward ceaselessly. Out along
the shoreline where a spit of sand curved round
to form a bay, half-hidden by a screen
of bushes, seven gulls stood lined up for
inspection, and each one immaculate
in plumage, white of breast with pearl-grey wings.
The boy moved not at all but waited till
his father, with his mother close behind,

stood silently beside him, three of them
together lost in time, beholding what
was there before them — just a row of gulls
whose forms were clean and pure against the brown
and greenish river rushing by. And then
as if at some one moment prearranged,
the gulls arced out their graceful wings and one
by one in winnowed flight gained liftoff from
the sandbar, drifting on to either side,
still low above the water. Mirror-like,
the surface caught each gull, developing,
apparently, an image from within
the depths, thrust deeper still (as every gull
gained height) until the "birds" had disappeared
beneath the shoreline — where the watchers stood.

The boy glanced sideways, then looked to the cope
of sky above them, back down at his feet.
He shrugged away a feeling that he had
and started walking slowly, paused, and now
reflected where the fishing should be best —
the stony shore beside the cooling spring,
or curving stretch of sand? Then choosing one

locale — although the other seemed as good
a choice — he hurried there; his parents came
more leisurely. The mother soon had spread
a blanket on the grass on which to sit
and read a rural weekly, looking up
now and again to watch her menfolk (as
already said, the boy was almost eight).

Quickly the boy began the ritual
of fishing, fumbling at the tackle — thick
hand lines whose board reels bounded up and down
like yo-yos in unravelling — securing
one line to a fresh-sharpened willow rod
forced deep into the mud, then flinging all —
stone sinker, baited hooks, and arcing line —
into the gliding current. For his part,
the father sat upon a rock right at
the water's edge, remembering, and found
vicarious enjoyment in his boy's
activity. He simply sat, bare feet
within the water's coolness, pressing soles
into the pebbly mud, content to have
time and the river here control his day.

After a while he'd try his luck at fishing—
yet let the boy catch one fish first. The boy
sat with the line untied, instead held it
between his fingers, hoping for a strike.
It seemed he was communicating with
the underwater world, atune to each
vibration being sent along the line
that linked him now with nature. Even a
transparent, gleaming dragonfly, alight
upon that part of line that rose above
the water, could be felt.

      Throughout the course
of the short afternoon, some fish were caught
by both the man and boy — gulls, winging by,
turned heads slantwise to see but did not slow
their cleaving flight. And as the day wore on,
the woman spread the picnic lunch upon
the blanket. Thoreau, speaking of wild apples,
once said that they should best be eaten in
the wind, outdoors, so all the senses, and
not just the taste, be fed. The woman, man,
and boy had, to accompany the meal,

the sound of water's purling flow, the keen
moist scent exuding from wet sand and from
luxuriance of growth along the shores,
the fine firm feel of earth to sit upon,
the panoramic view afforded by
the river's flatness with the opposite
receding bank in the warm, tawny light
of the departing day. The outing would
soon end, but it was pleasant yet to sit
and linger in the coolness and to watch
the shadows lengthen out across the water.
Both man and boy sat with their legs hunched up,
chins resting on their knees; the woman leaned
back, using arms as props — all staring at
the silent river flowing there before
them, ever changing, always still the same.

When finally the breadth of water lay
entirely in shadow, then the man
got up to gather in his tackle and,
while crouching at the shoreline, started in
to clean the fish he'd caught; the woman set
the picnic things aside; the boy left out

his land line (for a fish might yet be caught),
but knew he also had his catch to clean.
As he began to do so, he became
aware of gulls somehow materialized
above them, now no longer distant, dumb,
but funnelling about within a long
arm's reach. The birds were raucous, squabbling with
each other, fluttering in flight, astir
with their own singular persistence to
pick up the refuse of the fish — in haste
as if when dropping down they'd come upon
a swarm of locusts just alit out on
a farmer's field. Then when the leavings all
were gone, the gulls, all mute, dispersed — and were
gone, too.

And so with buggy packed, the horse
hitched up, the man, the woman, and the boy
began their winding trek slowly out of
the river valley. When on looking back,
they saw that the whole world below was one
of greenish tone: the shadowed water, a
deep, murky green; the wooded banks, long slopes

of what seemed blackish verdant furze; the sky
behind, a luminous blue apple-green.
One lone, high-flying gull appeared against
the river hills, whose recesses showed bits
of violet and purple. The bird caught
the sunlight on its yellowed wings — so clean
and pure, its stuff could not be sullied, while
it stroked a level homeward course within
the darkened valley.

           As the buggy now
emerged onto the open prairie, the
three occupants, somewhat surprised (although
they might have known, had they thought about
the matter), found they were yet once again
in the hot, sunlit land — the sun was still
an hour's time from setting. Here fields beside
the road continued to be parched, that year's
new growth a faded brown; the ditches had
wind-rippled drifts of soil, and dust from them
was thrown up in unnerving swirls by the
subsiding wind. The sounds of travel — wheels
slowly chirring through sand, the horse's hooves

falling dully upon the road — all these
gained resonance as evening soon came on.
The sun went down, a merciful event,
and left the western sky ablaze — reds, golds
suffused in glory — and the faces of
the three returning, man and wife and boy,
were painted in its light.

                    So going on,
they came into their yard at last, where the
bright glow had given way to mellow dusk,
the scattered buildings looming just above
the skyline, with the upper reaches' rose
becoming blue and darker indigo.
Chores quickly needed to be done — cows milked,
after a smudge was made, the cattle troughs
refilled with water (this the boy did at
the well across the pasture), other stock
attended to in preparation for
the nighttime. It was dark before the man and boy
went to the house — the woman had gone there
already. Now the coal-oil lamp was lit,
some fish were fried, and soon the three sat round

the table. The dim light gave closeness to
the setting — but a family at meal
together, talking with a few words of
their day.

       Much later in the evening's lull,
the lamp turned down, the man stepped out, before
retiring, to gauge the weather for
the coming day. The air still smelled of dust,
mixed now with not unpleasant farmyard odours —
the grass turned brown, for one — there was no dew
upon it. The wind was down, the sky above
still clear. A myriad of stars shone forth
palely, for a round moon was dominant
in the great curve of overarching sky —
its form and outline clean, distinct, in the
dry prairie air; its shining whiteness pure,
pre-Galilean, giving both the yard
and the outlying fields, with the dried grass
or crop upon them, now a silver look.
He saw the disc left standing at the field's
near corner, its round blades now gleaming in
the silver light. He thought of that day's work,

that afternoon's adventure with the gulls'
persistent presence. And before he turned
to go into the house, he thought of his
own family that night about the table.
He thought of wife inside, their boy asleep —
tomorrow he'd begin his work again.

FALL

LEAF FIRE

Flames —
snapping out,
licking the night's soft velvet,
curving the plastic dark —
issue a frail creeping smoke
that twists within itself
and disappears.

An old man stands guard,
resting on a rake.
Lost in thought,
he gazes at the fire
and at each smoking flame
that slowly dies.
Lost in thought,
he nonetheless must know
that his frail life creeps to its end
and soon must
flicker
out.

Mother braiding onions in the fall.

THE MEADOW

A late fall day I strolled out after chores
to gain a meadow where I'd been before;
the quiet sky was dull grey overcast,
the night impending. In the prolonged dusk
I reached the meadow's rim — and started through.
About me then the sober sky flushed rose
(a line of amber marked its western edge).
The land took on an unreal ruddy tone;
my meadow shone in richness, grasses of
medallion gold and sedges burnished bronze.
Enthralled, I stopped, beheld the wealth before
me long and long: the glowing carpets of
the sunset here below, the changing rust
and crimson sky above. All lost, I lingered,
waiting for what I could not tell — the hues
of sunset clutched, some wonderland traversed,
a glimpse into supernal things.

                                      Then, strange,
distracted thus, I found myself afoot
and walking homeward, though the sky retained

a waning evening light. And I turned round,
retraced my steps to that same meadow where
I'd been before — to try once more to clutch,
traverse, or glimpse that something that had been
there once, or may have been, or could be now.
I wandered slowly (deliberate
my course) while wraiths of mist rose from the grass,
and I looked keenly all about. The sky
grew dark, the meadow lands yet darker still,
the only movement one small darting bird,
which sought safe haven in the blackened sedge.

Time was unbribed: life's greatest sweetness, I
discovered, comes unbidden. Then I made
a second turn and strolled towards home again.

SAWING THE WINTER'S FUEL

Although the day was warm, the boy knew that
the winter soon would come. For several
past weeks, his father and his brother had
been hauling logs from out the pasture woods —
dried poplar for the most part, aspen and
some balsam, also an occasional
gnarled willow, grey with cores of orange-red
(this where an axe with slanted blow had struck).
Except for this one slash of brightness, all
the deadfall gathered pleased the eye with shades
of weathered browns, pale greens, and faded tans —
the colours comforting and of the earth.
The choppers worked within the shelter of
the woods, hewed at the forest refuse, cut
off branches, carried logs, and those they could
not carry, rolled by crowbar-saplings to
the clearing.

            There a team of horses stood,
cropping the pasture grass, and looked up when
the men appeared, the harness giving one

brief jingle. The Bain wagon, boxless, with
some logs already on it, rumbled up
as horses answered to the father's call
(it might have been a blackbird's *chucking* note)
and drew alongside logs that were for loading.
The father and the brother gripped one log
between them, each an end, and swung it high
upon the wagon, careful that a hand
would not be caught on stub or roughened bark.
The brother wore cloth gloves, the father, he
of older generation, worked barehanded.
With heavy logs, those rolled from out the bush,
two men were needed at each end so that
each end was lifted singly. Once again
great care was taken to prevent a hand
from being jammed between the twisted logs.
When a high flock of geese winged southward, swift
beneath the greying sky, the men stopped what
they did and watched the flight pass from their view
beyond the treetops' edge (the honking still
came to them softly), and, without a word,
fell to their work again.

Hauling logs for later sawing as winter's fuel. Author's father is at right.

                    Thus load on load
was made and drawn with creaking wheels into
the yard and each flung off to make in time
a massive pile in that one place reserved
for it, the farmyard's very centre. In
the months to come, the wood would take on prime
importance. Standing in the open door,
the boy, now just come home from school, watched the
proceedings. What was taking many days
to cut and haul and pile would be transformed
to yet another kind of heap in but
a single day — he flexed his hands, knowing
that he'd be called upon that day to help.
When the boy's father and his brother had
once hauled the last log home, the weather turned
much milder still, for Indian summer days
had come: chill mornings, frost on the pale grass,
and placid afternoons, warm, with clear skies.
The pasture woods' ruffed grouse, cock of drab browns
and faded tans, like those of deadfall and
the earth, resumed his autumn drumming where
the woods concealed him — stood upon a log
on which he had not drummed before (his old

stout log now lay within the farmer's yard).
The other gathered logs just lay there, too,
waiting ..., or so it seemed. The boy looked at
the pile each day when he walked off to school
and saw it bulking there each day on his
return. The autumn days continued mild.

And then one morning, snow was in the air;
small flakes came drifting from an overcast
so heavy it appeared that night was coming.
It snowed all day, not much, but at its close
the ground was white as one schoolboy trudged home.
The coming weekend they would saw the wood.
On Saturday, just after breakfast, all
the men (two and a boy, to be precise),
stamped out of doors, in doubled trousers and
thick mackinaws for warmth, and mitts or gloves
(the father now included) for the hands.
The week's sifting of snow crunched as they walked.
At the log pile the saw stood ready, its
round blade poised on a frame, completely open
so that no chip of wood might jam it. Soon
the blade began its whirring; the teeth,

its jagged outer edge, became a blur —
a popping stationary engine gave
more volume to the din.

                        The sawyers all
took up their stations: older brother at
the pile to drag up logs, the father at
the saw, the boy beside the whirring blade.
The first log slid along the frame until
it jutted past the blade by one stove-length.
(The wood once sawed would feed the kitchen range
and parlour heater.) The father pushed
the log into the blade — again ... again ... again —
each time to saw a one-foot length of wood.
Each time the boy, with mittened hands, grasped at
the end of log and followed its slow passage
into the cruel, sharp relentless blade,
and then each time, again, tossed the short length
of wood aside behind him. Thus the year's
new woodpile had its start — and this new day
its pattern. Endlessly all morning the
round blade sang still a high-pitched whine, that rose
in pitch in chipping through the log, and when

the log came free, changed to a twang, as from
a giant tuning fork: "Whir — whi-ine — twang!
Whir — whi-ine — twang!" The noise tore at one's brain,
even as the saw's blade sliced through each log.
(If geese passed overhead, no one could hear.)
It was relief when dinnertime came round.

The three of them slumped to the house and had
their quiet meal — the boy half-wishing it
were longer, and half-wishing that the end
of all the sawing had not been delayed.
They rose, as at a signal, and went out,
back to their work. The engine popped once more,
the blade whirred to its high-pitched whine, and logs
came end on end. "Why couldn't what was left
be left for yet another day?" the boy
mused to himself. "And couldn't workers who
were morning-fresh do more in morning hours?"
Such were his thoughts as still his brother dragged
up log upon another log, and as
his father pushed repeatedly each log
to biting blade: "Whir — whi-ine — twang!" The boy
now hoped the work for once and all would end
that day.

Always his hands were just a few
scant inches from the saw. He never ceased,
could never cease, his concentration — a
monotony of watching hands, the blade;
then throwing wood away; grasping the log
again; a reaching always to the blade,
again and yet again, but not too close.
A weary watching, throwing, grasping, as
the pile of logs diminished and the pile
of wood grew high behind him. Sometimes when
the blade struck at a knot, the father jerked
the log away so that the saw would not
get stuck and stop — a break for all of them,
a needed coming to their senses as
the saw would sing at yet another pitch
if only for an instant (but the end
of log might twist and bring one's hands within
an even closer distance to the blade).
Or the small looping belt might slip off the
saw's pulley. Then the boy could step back from
the blade and let his mind relax for one
brief minute, only to approach the saw
once more and then resume the sawing. When
a log, however straight and free of knots,

was huge (the grouse's log), the boy just could
not throw the heavy lengths away — he thrust
them merely to the side and watched so that
their presence there would not cause him to trip.
And as the pile behind him grew, he had
to be on guard for pieces rolling down
the pile and towards his feet.

                                 A seemingly
eternal vigilance was paid — and it
was needed to be paid — to make the day
successful. For the boy had pictures in
his mind of other years: his father's fainting at
the saw, his wavering — and falling *back*
into the snow; a neighbour's hurried trip
by horse and stoneboat into town —*his* son,
hand wrapped in cloths spotted with blood. The boy
could not but help to steel himself to be
alert. And so the long day's work proceeded.
Log after log was sawed — the whirring blade
continuing its song — piece after piece of wood
was added to the pile.

                    Then finally
the older brother dragged the last log to
the saw. No time for exultation now,
although the father glanced down at the boy.
This roughened log must yet be cut with that
deliberate, painstaking care as were
the others. When the whining ceased — the log
was sawed, the last piece thrown aside — the blade
still spun with menace. Then the quiet boy,
unmoving, watched it till his father stopped
the engine, till the blur of teeth grew clear,
and till the driving belt was taken off.
So up to then the boy just stood there, numb
and only then he backed away in safety.

A strange silence ensued, the air about
was suddenly so quiet that all three
companions just stood by and looked, not at
each other. To their ears there came a rush
of little sounds, now magnified, the wind
in leafless pasture trees, a small bird's wings
in flight. The boy, relieved in feeling, walked
around the winter's horde of wood. He had
his satisfaction, too, thinking ahead

to colder days. It was a pleasure now
to walk around the pile, engaging in
the safer work of throwing errant pieces
that lay around the edge high up onto
the pile so that this store of fuel would
shed rain and snow the better.

                              To the boy
the day's tense occupation would be soon
forgotten — till remembered as the long
ago a full year later. Even when
it came time to fill the woodbox in the porch,
in crouching down to fill his upheld arm,
he would reflect upon the warm earth tones
of woodpile dark against the winter's snow,
without a thought of one hard previous
day's sawing (it was but a job to do).
If anything, the autumn memories
to come to him would be recalled of what
his father and his older brother had
described — of wild geese calling softly high
above the treetops and of one ruffed grouse,
earth-coloured, stepping off his drumming log
and slipping from their view through underbrush.

WINTER

Grey overcast cover, sombre, drab —
set closing of November days,
the silent low sky dim,
oppressing, darker even
than the cold slate-greyish snow;

stark trees, a frosty interstitial haze
and shadowed depths, moveless,
with dusk upon them — a standing gloom
(the old weaponry of winter leashed)
and threshold of contending night.

                                     Then,
a thinness in the dark cloud cover,
a paling in the west, a russet seeping
through the pall of greyishness —
a smudge of lurid crimson,
smoldering above the snow;

brief searing weld of sky and earth —
soon, lustreless and black, obliterated,
hidden in the shadows,
and quietly effaced
by night's swift catapult.

SURVIVAL

Partridges
pocketed in bluish snow
uneasy at my coming
take sudden wing
cackling alarm notes
fluttering noisily,
then falling into low formation
sail in graceful arch-winged curves
(silent airships, rusty-red, in missiled flight)
to snowy cover elsewhere.

The ski trail started from the farmhouse where
the young boy lived and radiated out
in parallel straight lines (that is, at first)—
a plane geometry embossed in snow —
each double radii extending in
that one direction that the boy that day
had freshly made. Outside the door the skis,
when not in use, were stuck into a snowdrift,
the very snow that always was well-banked
against the house for insulation. By
late afternoon, with lessons done — the boy
was studying at home in winter and
postponed his recesses till then — he slipped
into his skis, homemade with single toe-straps,
and so began the real adventure of
the day — to snowy woods and pastures new.

And yet there was no destination, just
a setting out and then a random course,
skiing out of the way to see a ridge
of snow or stopping on a rise of land

to let his eyes sweep all around along
the grey horizon, with the day itself
dictating what was done. A rabbit's tracks,
dice patterns in the snow, were there to follow,
and almost certainly, somewhere a flock
of sharp-tailed grouse, plump birds caught feeding on
some weedstalks, startled into sudden flight,
surprised into a whirring clattering
of wings, then kite-like sailing in a stream
of air, over a hill and out of sight —
giving both life and colour (tawny brown)
to what was otherwise a seemingly
cold, still, and sterile landscape.

                             The best time
to ski, the young boy learned, was after storm
on storm had shaped the snow into hard drifts —
late February, early March — and his
scant weight was easily supported. What
he liked still more, however, was the way
the drifts were sculpted, honed into a mix
of surfaces — ribbed slopes and crested peaks
and swerving dunes and undulating plains.

Each type of cover added zest to all
his skiing ventures, an indulging of
his kinesthetic sense (if he but knew),
a feeling of leg muscles working as
each new terrain demanded — and the world
experienced in simple fashion.

But

it was the subtle tints of textured snow —
for snow is hardly ever white — that was
his greatest interest. These were prevalent
in light that lingered with the lengthening
of days. And as the sun sank towards the skyline,
the snow became more blue, and deeper blue,
reflecting darkening blue heights above,
yet marvellously complementing reds
and dusky oranges within the west.
Some slopes of snow revealed a pinkish cast
for one brief interval and then gave way
to woad and indigo, maintaining still
some blueness even later into twilight.

The boy had wandered now on skis up to
a straw stack left from threshing in the fall.

It loomed above the azure fields, a hill
of amethystine shadow, yellowed by
protruding tufts of straw in sunset's glow.
Here was his downhill ski run, not to be
resisted. Up he climbed with skis kicked off
and tucked beneath an arm, but then he had
to reconnoitre — which sloped side to first
assay? He found it best to sit down on
his skis, toboggan-fashion, and push off
to gain a better notion of the slope
and of its foibles, for some strawy tufts
might hook a ski away beneath him. Then
there would not be the parallel straight lines;
repairs would be required.

                    Now at last
he dared to try, to *stand* upon his skis
upright and poised for swishing, headlong flight,
his upper body slanting forward. Yet
he looked across the silent landscape, saw
the fields ashimmer in the day's last light,
and leaped ahead, into the frosty wind
now streaming by, a kite-like swoop, and swift,

adown the stack and sailing on, and on,
and then a coming to a stop, his breath
once more a cloud before his face as he
breathed deeply (seemed he'd left off breathing for
an instant).

       Stepping out a pattern, just
like radii in a half circle (that
geometry again), he turned his skis
back to the straw stack, and, once there, climbed up
its slope in order to repeat his past
performance — many times. A whitish moon,
new-risen, moved in space, and climbed its sky,
turning the winter world to silver, and
one boy enjoyed himself, with silver wings
to course his downhill run of snow and straw —
the snow crunched ever louder in the still
night air.

       Then finally the boy turned home.
Another light, a coal-oil lamp, shone from
its window, and its curling moonlit smoke
rose slowly upward. It was good to burst

into the warm confines of living room
and kitchen, with his supper waiting there,
while knowing that his homemade skis (his own
mercurial bright wings) wcre safely left
outside, and ready to be used again
on further carefree jaunts another day.

AFTERWORD

Anna Friesen: 1899-1988

I

Now when my mother had been married for
some months, in idle conversation — or
it may have been a girlish ruse to please
or otherwise impress her older husband —
she started to describe a certain kind
of flower that she'd known from childhood. It
had grown wild among wild grasses where the straight,
white aspen poplar left small open patches
of saline dampness — these above the beach
and weeded margins of a saline lake.
"Like little moccasins," she said, "the shape
of footwear that an Indian of old
would wear" (my mother once had found a great
grey-coloured arrowhead along this lake
while going for the cows — indeed, it lay
within the water-filling hoofprint of
a cow — so Indians were on her mind).
"Its flower was the moccasin, a bunched
together blossom, hollow for a foot,
a tiny, tiny foot to slip in — and
all yellow."

Now, she did not know that it
was called a "lady's slipper," even though
she said a foot might "slip in"—la-de-da!
No lady that she knew (the only ones
she'd ever met were in some book and those
within a fairy tale) would deem to wear
a shoe like that. What "ladies" wore were shoes,
as everybody knew, with pointed toes
and arching heels—real slippers made of glass
or satin. Maybe some stout Dutchman might
compare these yellow flowers to his *klompen*—
but to a "lady's slipper" never. Thus
my mother with her peasant, pioneer
upbringing would have soon dismissed the name.

My father listened with a bemused smile,
protesting somewhat—"Now, dear girl ...." He knew,
he said (in a superior tone, his age
already standing in good stead), that all
the flowers hereabout that he had seen
had petals—they were what made flowers flowers!
Small moccasins on flowers—no, indeed—
just who in all his life had heard of such
a thing? He hadn't.

It was then his glance
at her cut short his talk. Her whitened face
was almost giving way to tears. Was she
in earnest then, her softly spoken words
made light of by his male unthinkingness?
Still, moccasin-type flowers! Or was she
once more — he never could be sure, it seemed
(he glanced a second time at her young face —
he did not want to stare),...was she, as she
was wont to do, but having female fun
at his expense (his age again?)— and was this fun
in part, the fact of his uncertainty?
Better for him to let the matter drop.

A year or two, with nothing said of these
small yellow lady's slippers, lapsed, and then
my mother and my father chanced to be
invited to another farm home. There
in bold display upon a table was
a bowl of yellow flowers picked nearby.
Each flower was a moccasin, a bunched
together blossom. "Come," my mother said,
"and look. For these are just the ones I meant."

It seemed their conversation of a year
or two ago had never discontinued.
She stood beside the flowers, waiting for
my father, bent to touch the precious footwear;
plain Indian or Dutch design they were
despite the designation —"lady's slipper."
My father looked and wondered well at what
he saw — and saw with now a sideways glance
delight upon his young wife's face: she had
her vindication. Yet another glance
(he stared this time and knew) revealed that that
was not her joy — his being older told
him once what he was certain to be true.
She had described the flowers out of love
for them, for him, for childhood faithfully
remembered, and now here in love relived.
They were for all to see and to behold.

All this is but preamble to a further
love: that however much my mother liked
the lady's slipper — call it what you will,
the flower known from early childhood years —

the plant was not her favourite among
the flowers; prairie roses were! She had
a passion for them — pink and darker rose
and red — for really any tint of red
was grand ovation for her, speaking to
her blood, transporting her in quiet joy,
the colour of colours incredible,
that spoke of life that stirred within. In the
naïveté of childhood there was but
one colour for her — red! (She had a kind
of synthetic sensibility
to see within her mind her sisters' names
each in distinctive shape and colour — and
her own name, Anna, was a great red heart.)

The red, red rose was then her flower of
all flowers, wild in growth and growing in
wild places. Natural it was when she
in early marriage bore a daughter, then
to name her for the flower, honouring
them both, expressing love that would not let
them go. My mother in sweet solace had
a rose in winter then, reminding her

of summer roses. What a brief time a rose
does flourish, even such a winter rose
upon her knee: she died in a year's time.
Only a mother who has lost a child
could know my mother's grief, could know the kind
and gentle way that grief is set aside,
locked up within the secret heart or mind
when other children come — it never dies:
always for Mother, with her passion for
the flower, seeing prairie roses bloom
each glorious June in fragrant roadside splendour;
always another rose remembered in
the pathway of her mind.

                    Some sixty-five
years later, Mother lying weak upon
her bed, spoke of a dream she dreamed
one night before, of little Rosie just
as once she was. For her it must have been
a lovely dream to see her daughter there.
And this occurred short days before she died
herself, died suddenly within the month
of June, succumbed when daytime heat had brought

the roses out — rare pink and darker rose
and red — resplendent far afield but yet
dear roses that she never saw — only
a rose seen clearly in a dream, beheld
for one brief instant, then held lovingly
within her secret heart and mind — dear Mother!

But I was not yet done with lady's slippers.
For when my mother died — it was a day
or two thereafter — to assuage the ache
for days that were and would not be again, that
I, lonely, wandered through the pasture land
of our small farm. Scrub bush and prairie it
had been when Mother and my father moved
there, newly married. They had walked across
each acre, planning fields and farmyard, knew
and cherished every foot of ground there was.
Just so, as children, we had scrambled through
each dip or valley, also over all
the hillsides so that nothing nature offered —
a secret bird's nest or new flower — could
escape our fond attention. Then the years

that followed saw me still continuing
my pasture strolls, upon familiar ground
yet once again, always with something of
my boyish gladness still intact and with
a thankfulness for country things.

         On this
occasion, slowly walking, while old thoughts
came tumbling in upon me, I resumed
my customary circuit, noting grass
and trees and mix of clouds but vaguely — yet,
there was a comfort in these things seen with
abstracted eye, while in my mind revolved
remembrances of yesterdays, now long
ago, and questionings on life cut short.
My walk became more hurried. Suddenly,
my absent gaze grew sharp, reflections stopped —
before me, at my feet, where never there
had been in all my years, or in the years
of both my parents, there amid the grass
were yellow lady's slippers, just one plant
beside the nearby overarching trees,
small blossoms bright beneath the clouded sky.

These lady's slippers were found growing on the farm, 1988.

I crouched before them, wondered at their rare
appearance —"moccasins" or "Dutchmen's *klompen*,"
my mother's flowers known to her from childhood.
The ache I felt (and still continued then
to feel) for what was lost to me through one
great heart not beating, was to be allied,
I knew, forever, with this day and with
these flowers blooming. And the sense of what
was gone and not to be again, might gain
an aureole of grace and splendour now
that nature in a wise unanxious way
seemed to remember here a heart that loved.

Next day in twilight, I once more set out
along my pasture walk, seeking the peace
of soul that nature had afforded. Where
the lady's slippers grew, I stood and watched
day's ending come upon the land. Mists hung
in dips and hollows, sinuous before
the darkened trees; scents of damp grasses and
June roses filtered up through sweet, moist air;
the evening sky was still diffuse with warm,
soft light. And in this light I wandered on —

with longings, lady's slippers (roses too),
mulled in my mind along with nature's own
remembrance, seeming so, from yesterday —
when from the darkened trees ahead a deer
stepped out and waited, its great ears erect
and large eyes looking at me unafraid
(its rusty summer coat in dusk's dim light
was coloured like the redness of a rose).
I tried a hesitant slow step forward,
and, curious, it, too, advanced and stopped.
Two beings looking each to each, the deer
as nature's emissary showing in
its way that all was well, and would be well.
Composed, it walked along the clearing's edge
and then in graceful, splendid bounds was gone:
remembrance made (if not by nature, then
within my heart with love for what was lost
and dear) and now an affirmation given.

ABOUT THE AUTHOR

Victor Carl Friesen was born and raised on a small Saskatchewan farm when country living was still much the same as it had been for his parents in their childhood. Life, though hard, had abundant rewards. As Henry David Thoreau has said, "That man is richest whose pleasures are cheapest."

Friesen, in fact, would become a Thoreau specialist, focusing on the naturalist-philosopher in his graduate studies (M.A., University of Saskatchewan; Ph.D., University of Alberta). He has written two books on his specialty, as well as some dozen critical articles, and given a paper at Brock University, Ontario, on "Science, Spirituality, and the Environment" with relation to Thoreau.

Friesen has published more than 200 essays, articles, stories and poems in various journals and anthologies. His other books are on such diverse topics as Mennonite folklore (first winner of the Alberta Book of the Year Award) and a history of the Saskatchewan Rivers. *The Year Is a Circle* features his landscape photography. *The Gift of Country Life* is his seventh book, and second book of poetry.

The Spirit of the Huckleberry: Sensuousness In Henry Thoreau (Edmonton: University of Alberta Press, 1984)

The Mulberry Tree (with Anna Friesen) (Winnipeg: Queenston House, 1985) (Reprinted Saskatoon: Prairie Lily Books, 1997)

The Windmill Turning: Nursery Rhymes, Maxims and Other Expressions of Western Canadian Mennonites (Edmonton: University of Alberta Press, 1988)

The Year Is a Circle: A Celebration of Henry David Thoreau (Toronto: Natural Heritage, 1995; reprinted 1996 & 2002)

Where the River Runs: Stories of the Saskatchewan and the People Drawn to Its Shores (Calgary: Fifth House, 2001)

Forever Home: Good Old Days on the Farm (Calgary: Fifth House, 2004)

The Gift of Country Life (Toronto: Natural Heritage, 2005)